In memory of my parents:

Marge and Jerry Weissman

who supported and encouraged me to complete this project
and were always proud of my accomplishments.....PB

Sweet Dreams

Pat Britz

Animals Need Zzz's, Too
Discover the many ways You and Animals sleep

When do you sleep?

Where do you sleep?

How much sleep do you need?

How do you sleep?

How long do you sleep?

What happens during sleep?

With whom do you sleep?

Written by

Patricia A. Britz

Illustrated by

Kelly Carter

PK Publishing House, Vienna, VA

To my husband, Ken Britz, whose love, support and endless patience made this book possible,
and for contributing numerous creative sketches…..PB

⤸ NATIONAL SLEEP FOUNDATION

Special thanks to the National Sleep Foundation for making *Animals Need Zzz's, Too* available across the country.

The National Sleep Foundation is dedicated to improving sleep health and safety through education, public awareness, and advocacy. It is well-known for its annual *Sleep in America* poll.

The Foundation is a charitable, educational and scientific not-for-profit organization located in Washington, DC. Its membership includes researchers and clinicians focused on sleep medicine, professionals in the health, medical and science fields, individuals, patients, families affected by drowsy driving and more than 900 healthcare facilities throughout North America.

A heart-felt thanks goes out to Paul Wiegmann for his consultation and advice and to Mid Scanlon for help with editing this book.

Summary: Sleep is a universal and basic biological drive for both humans and animals. Each section of this book discusses an aspect of a child's sleep and compares how people sleep with the fascinating ways that animals sleep. Descriptions of sleep are based on sleep science.

Published by
PK Publishing House
Vienna, Virginia

ISBN-13: 978-0-615-65764-6/ISBN-10: 0615657648 (soft cover)

Library of Congress Control Number: 2012911103

Text and illustrations copyright © 2012 by PK Publishing House

Printed in the United States of America
First Edition

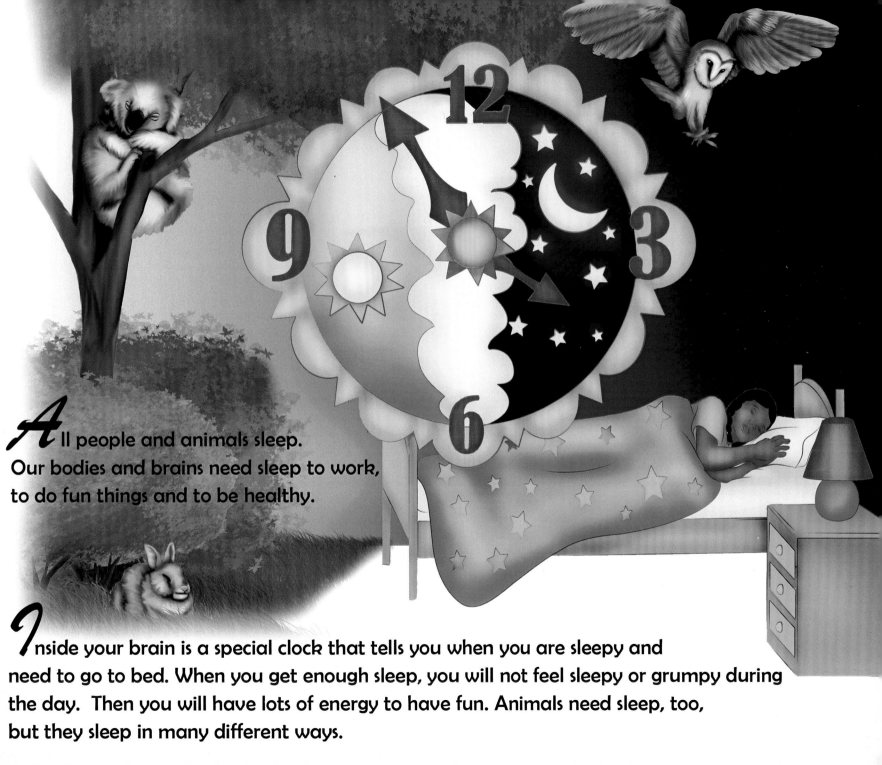

*A*ll people and animals sleep.
Our bodies and brains need sleep to work,
to do fun things and to be healthy.

*I*nside your brain is a special clock that tells you when you are sleepy and
need to go to bed. When you get enough sleep, you will not feel sleepy or grumpy during
the day. Then you will have lots of energy to have fun. Animals need sleep, too,
but they sleep in many different ways.

When do you sleep?
Is it light or dark outside?

*B*abies need lots of sleep. It helps them grow so they can get bigger.
Babies sleep during the day and at night.

*Y*oung children sleep a long time at night when it is dark.
Then they take naps during the day.
When you get older and go to school, you won't need to
grow so fast, so you will sleep mostly at night.

Some animals stay awake all night!
While you are sleeping, owls are awake,
flying about looking for food.
Have you ever heard an owl hoot when it is dark?

If you were in a forest at night, you might see a bat flying
round until morning, when it is ready to sleep. Far away,
gers roam at night and sleep during the day, too.

How much sleep do you need?
Think of opposites

*W*hen you are little, you need lots of sleep — up to 14 hours a day. Just like plants that need sun and water to grow, you need sleep to get bigger.

*A*s you get bigger and when you become a grown-up, you will need only seven or eight hours of sleep each night. Like grown-ups, most bigger animals need less sleep. Like children, smaller animals need more sleep.

If you or a friend has a cat, you probably have seen it sleeping.
Cats sleep a little, wake up and then sleep some more.
They can sleep up to 18 hours all through the day and night.

Have you seen a giraffe
at the zoo?
It is a big animal but it
only sleeps about two hours
each day – and it sleeps
standing up!
Can you do that?

*S*ome little animals like squirrels and hamste[rs] need many hours of sleep. Squirrels are out and about during the day, but they sleep for about 15 hours, often in a tree, where they are safe from danger.

*H*amsters sleep around 14 hours,
but mostly during the day.
They can be quite noisy at night, when
they are having fun and eating.

*C*ows and elephants are big
so they need just about four
hours of sleep every day.
Cows are very busy eating during the day.

How long do you sleep?

*N*aps: *Sleeping for a short time*

Babies and young children take naps because they need more sleep during the day. When a cat takes a short nap during the day, it is called a "cat nap."

Some animals only take naps, sleeping for a few minutes at a time. That is so they can always be on the lookout for danger.

Ken's Ostrich Farm

Rabbits take short naps so they can be ready to run quickly if an enemy is near. Ostriches are very good at napping. They sleep for no longer than 15 minutes at a time standing up, so they are ready to move quickly if they see danger.

Hibernation: *Sleeping for a long time*

Some animals hibernate, which means they go away
and sleep for a long time.
Often, their body temperature goes down
and they eat little or nothing while they hibernate.

*B*ears go into dens and sleep all winter.
Chipmunks curl into a furry ball underground.

Where do you sleep?
Inside or outside?

*P*eople usually sleep inside on a bed, a couch or sometimes in a chair.
If you have been camping you may have slept outside in a tent.
Your bed may be your favorite place to sleep.

Cats and dogs sleep anywhere – on a window sill, a rug, a couch or even outside on the grass. Some dogs and cats like sleeping with their owners.

Trees, Water, Caves
On and Underground

Most wild animals sleep outside where they live.
Animals have different kinds of homes and they can sleep
in strange places. Many are very good at making their own special beds.

*T*rees are a favorite place because animals can climb up high or go inside a tree to sleep and be safe. Would you like to sleep in a tree like a bird or monkey or koala?

If you could sleep in a tree, where would you sleep?
Chimpanzees and orangutans sleep on a branch.
Every night, orangutans make a new bed of branches and leaves.
They wrap their fingers and toes around the branch so they won't fall.
Chimpanzees wrap their tails around the branch.

Water is another favorite place to sleep. Have you ever seen a duck sleeping on a lake? In the ocean, sea otters make a bed of slippery, slimy seaweed and sleep on it. Covered with the seaweed, they can hide from sharks. The seaweed bed is also comfortable and it keeps the sea otter from drifting away.

*I*t must be cold to sleep on an iceberg! But not for a polar bear, which has a great coat to keep it warm. Could you sleep on ice in your winter coat?

*I*f you have gone camping, you may have slept in a sleeping bag on the ground. A parrotfish also makes a sleeping bag. It is a jelly-like bubble and the fish sleeps inside of it. The bubble floats in the water.

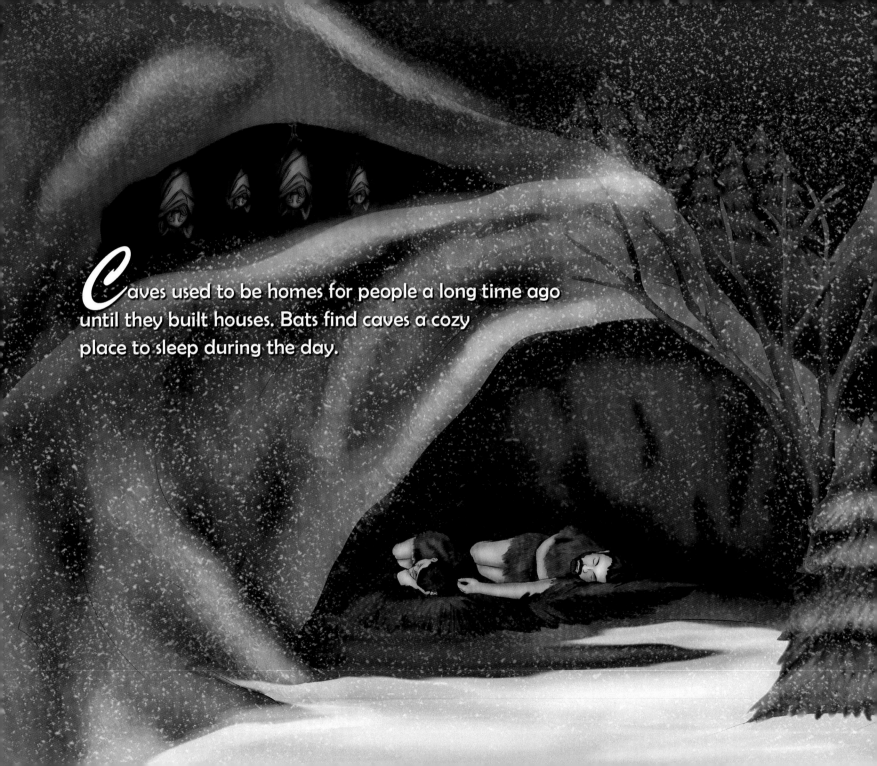

Caves used to be homes for people a long time ago until they built houses. Bats find caves a cozy place to sleep during the day.

Bears and mountain lions like to sleep in caves, too.
Would you like to sleep in a cave with a bear?

$\mathcal{U}$nderground is another favorite place for some
animals like prairie dogs. They dig tunnels for their sleeping place.
Rabbits sleep in little tunnels called burrows.
Frogs like to sleep in the mud.
Maybe they don't have to take baths!

How do you sleep?
Up or down?

*W*hat is your favorite way to sleep?

People sleep on their backs or sides or tummies in different positions,
but mostly they sleep lying down with their eyes closed.

Some animals sleep standing up. Some animals sleep upside down.

*D*id you ever try to sleep standing up? Adult penguins do, with their heads tucked under their wings. They often circle around their young to protect them from the cold and other animals. Elephants and horses and cows can sleep standing up, too.

Could you sleep standing up on just one leg?
That's what some pretty birds like herons and flamingos do.
They sleep with one leg tucked up under a wing – and they do not fall!
They might make good dancers.

Ducks sometimes stand in a row and tuck their heads under their feathers.

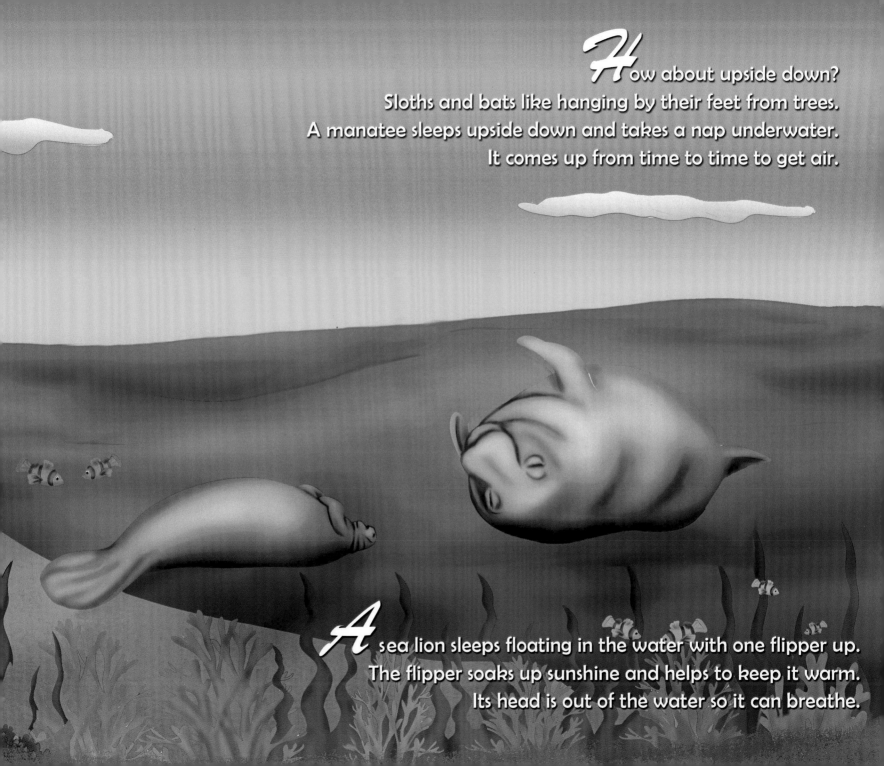

*H*ow about upside down?
Sloths and bats like hanging by their feet from trees.
A manatee sleeps upside down and takes a nap underwater.
It comes up from time to time to get air.

A sea lion sleeps floating in the water with one flipper up.
The flipper soaks up sunshine and helps to keep it warm.
Its head is out of the water so it can breathe.

A partridge sleeps on the ground with its legs up in the air.
Did you ever see a dog do that? Fish never close their eyes.
Do you know why? They have no eyelids. Can you sleep with your eyes open?

What happens during sleep?
Coos, colors and cooler

When people sleep, their brains are still working. People are not aware of what is going on outside their bodies. But, when dolphins sleep, just part of their brain is awake and another part is asleep.
The part that is awake is making sure that the dolphin goes to the surface to breathe and that there is no danger nearby.

*B*abies make a lot of noise when they sleep.
They coo, whimper and may even smile while sleeping.
All people have eye movements when they sleep.
This happens when we are dreaming.
Do you remember your dreams? Dreams can be fun or scary.

Many animals also dream and they make noise while they are sleeping. If you see a dog or cat twitching its paws or whiskers when sleeping, it may be dreaming.

neighhh...

Horses neigh in their sleep and elephants may twitch.
People who study sleep have found that songbirds dream of singing
and may be practicing during sleep. Even rats dream.
What do you think they dream about?

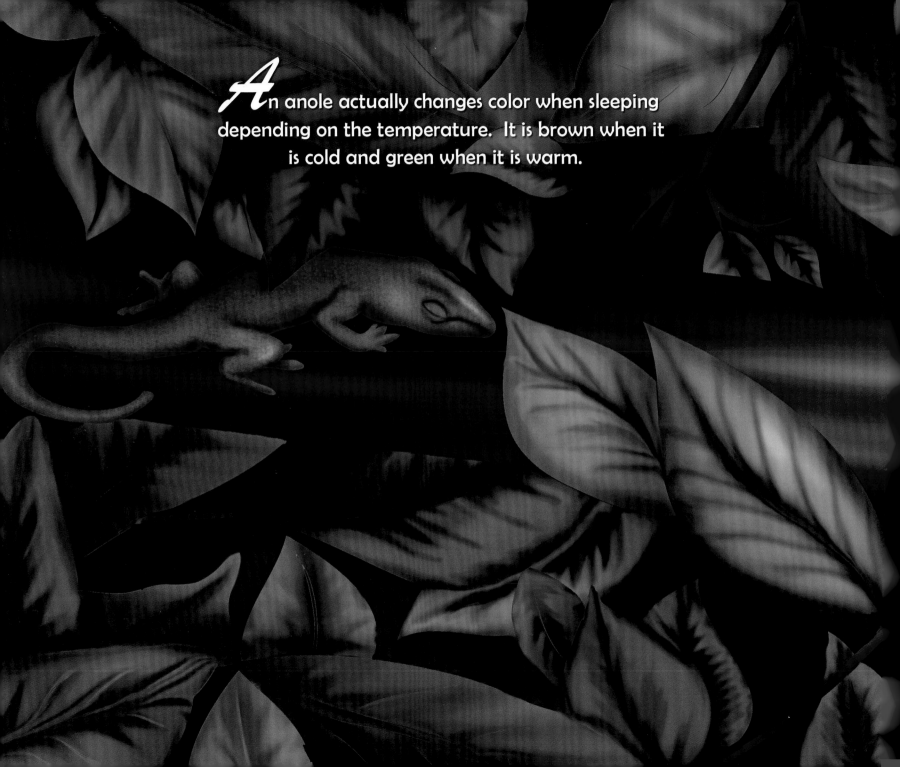

An anole actually changes color when sleeping depending on the temperature. It is brown when it is cold and green when it is warm.

*W*hat color would you like to be when you sleep?
You do not change color when you sleep, but your
body does get cooler. Maybe that is why we like to have a blanket to cover us.

With whom do you sleep?
Alone or with others?

Many animals sleep in groups.

Wild animals that sleep together also often travel together.

Animals like lions, monkeys, zebras and some insects like to sleep in groups.

Owl monkeys sleep with their long tails linked together. Can you wrap your arms and legs around someone and sleep?

Other animals prefer to be alone all the time except for special times such as when they are taking care of their young. Bobcats, moose, tigers and even some snakes like to sleep alone. Snakes like to curl up under a log.

Next time you go to the park, to the zoo or just outside in your neighborhood, look around for sleeping animals. You will see that they sleep in many ways.

*Good night:
Sleep well.*

Getting a good night's sleep is important

because when you sleep well, the next day you will feel good,

and be happy and ready to play.

For Parents: Tips for a Good Night's Sleep

- Set up a bedtime routine with your child. This can include brushing teeth, taking a bath, having a light snack, putting on pajamas and reading a book.

- Establish a regular bedtime for every night including weekends.

- Children should go to bed when they begin to feel tired. Encourage your child to fall asleep on his or her own.

- A child's bedroom should be quiet and at a comfortable temperature with little or no light. It is best not to have a TV or video on at bedtime.

- A child should have the same sleep environment all night.

Visit the National Sleep Foundation website: www.sleepfoundation.org

Patricia A. Britz
BIOGRAPHY

Ms. Britz was Program Director at the National Sleep Foundation (NSF) for seven years, where she wrote numerous articles and public education brochures on sleep, presented at national professional and scientific meetings, and lectured at state and local school board meetings. She developed NSF's website, "Sleep for Kids" and made presentations on establishing healthy sleep habits in children for over 500 sleep centers across the country.

Patricia Britz has Master degrees in Education and in Public Management with a focus on health from Carnegie-Mellon University. For over 30 years, she has developed professional literature and programs on health-related topics for patients and the public. She has also co-authored scientific journal articles on sleep-related topics such as insomnia, sleep apnea and restless legs syndrome.

Pat enjoys spending time with her six grandchildren, making up new stories and reading books together. She currently lives with her husband in northern Virginia.

Kelly Carter
BIOGRAPHY

Ms. Carter is a graduate of Northern Michigan University in Marquette, Michigan where she obtained her Bachelor's degree in Art & Design. In 2005 Ms. Carter started Mad Spider Studio, a professional illustration and graphic design business. Ms. Carter's artwork can be found in children's books, greeting cards, children's educational products, and book covers.

For more information visit her website at www.madspiderstudio.com.